JUSTICE

Also by Caroline Finkelstein

Windows Facing East
Germany

Caroline Finkelstein

Caroline Finkelstein

JUSTICE

1975   1999

Twenty-Five Years of Publishing
Carnegie Mellon University Press

Acknowledgments

Poems in this book have appeared, sometimes in different format, in the following magazines: *American Poetry Review, Borderlands, The Georgia Review, The Gettysburg Review, Harvard Magazine, The Onset Review, Ploughshares* and *Poetry*.

I wish to thank Louis Asekoff, Donald Hall, Joyce Peseroff and Ellen Bryant Voigt for their help with the manuscript of *Justice*.

And again, I wish to thank The MacDowell Colony.

The publication of this book is supported by a grant from the Pennsylvania Council on the Arts.

Library of Congress Catalog Card Number 97-76755
ISBN 0-88748-297-X Pbk.
Copyright © 1999 by Caroline Finkelstein
Printed and bound in the United States of America

10 9 8 7 6 5 4 3 2 1

Contents

I

II

III

For Nicholas

I

AT THE EQUINOX

The minor-key conclusions of dim rooms stop killing me.

One fish grey day follows one so clear and colorful.
My mother's bugle-beaded ghost quits; I can't imagine her

unglamorous, yet she's hiking up to Broadway
without her demi-world retinue, it's just 90th street,

dirty where the kids play the music of the texture
of their bodies and their silken ribbons

hung with skate keys. It's a Saturday afternoon
some years after one old woman died.

Charity takes me and leaves me as the asters flower,
as the part-dark self my son is emerges greedily hungry,

as the lane I'm on leaves dawn, bends, returns, amends
as the shift within begins.

FABRIC

In the book there is a page for
the Empress again.

She is so beautiful, so serious
cultivating silk.

The nobility follow her example,
raising chewing worms that spit

mulberry leaves in perfumed rooms.

The lovely Empress,

her countrymen credit her
with the invention of the loom and reeling silk.

Chinese literature testifies to this.

In the second millennium B.C.,
silk becomes the Chinese money

and any dolt who has a knack
with worms and horticulture

makes a fortune in the export business.

When I close my eyes and find my father
folding piece goods by his pushcart

it is Mulberry Street and 1920.

My hungry father folding silk
thinks of heaven, thinks of plums,

then walks through Chinese laundry steam
into courtyards full of women

good and still, and fixed by sex.
In the book the girls are

exhibited, on moonlit lawns,
fluttering excitedly

like bodies taught to copy moths.

And the mandarin sits watching —

all of us sit watching, human
pleasure being what it is.

I WANTED TO FORGET

The Maestro, my mother's
singing teacher,
how he hissed
the words behind his bad false teeth:
slowly, darling, softly,
darling Tosca,
for God's sake, who invited him
into my shadows,
that bald, fat man?

I wanted to stuff my ears,
shut myself away
from his thick wrist hairs
and glasses
in the pocket of
his shirt so clearly European.
Once the Germans had him
walking naked
through the station in Vienna.

I wanted to forget
the moderately ambitious
humans buying bread,
collecting furniture and
idiotic postcards,
and what they were wearing
and if they were lawyers
and who had daughters, and how
they were fed to the pigs.

Tosca, darling. I shuddered
listening to those
whistling teeth and heavy breaths
sobbing scales. And lived
like that for years, ordinary

in my dream: a perfect circle
of a pink felt skirt, pockets
filled with tickets
to the newest musical.

IS THAT THE WIND RATTLING A TIN PLATE AGAIN?

The four-hands concerto they practiced on the child,
those shades in human form, they said

the child dreamed it, dreamed that rapid music
beneath her chest and belly, dreamed the pulse, the bed,

the death of daylight, four p.m., the silence, wild silence

followed by the clink, the dropped syringe, the

laughing, unconfused and focused dreadful laughing.
And if obsessive figures still are shadows in her

dizzy head, morning penetrates

her heart that lures you
with its tutored art and boom and gush.

And avid red —

SYMPATHY

We had a store, a house, a maid.
That's how it was. That's how it was.

We had a maid. She scrubbed our stains.
We're Jews; we'd been through hell.
We had a maid; she was very light.
She'd been through hell; we knew.

We had a discount store; we *invented* discount;
we had a maid who was almost white; she swabbed.
We had a car. We'd ride to New Rochelle
to see our brother and his wife;

they had a store; they rivaled us.

We had a store; we'd been through hell;
it was murder with the union;
we wanted peace but the police called up:
we got a woman here; her name is Loma,

claims she cleans for you . . .

they found her drunk on the I.R.T.
They said she blamed her menopause.

Menopause, my ass!

We had a maid who fell down drunk.
Her beautiful daughter came to us
to get her mother's uniforms.
We thought she looked like Lena Horne.

Lena Horne, our mother said:
they wouldn't let her use the bathroom.

We had a store, a house and books; we're Jews;
we had a history of books, of buying books.
We had a history of hell: beds of straw, straw and piss.
We had a maid. Imagine that. Imagine that.

She ironed our shirts. She washed our sweat.
She drank. She fell. Her daughter came.

You Jews! she said. Imagine that. That's how it was.

PORTRAIT AND PRINTS

Here is Mary Cassatt flattening the plane,
Mary Cassatt in a book in New Hampshire.

The landscape is March, flinty sky
all over the place, and weakness, and wisdom.

Right now, no petals
fall on the lawns, no luxury

rots in the grass; the art of tomorrow
keeps hidden. When I walk anywhere

I see her Japanese greens
the birches throw light on: spruce

and hemlock and pine.

Her parents forbade her so much —
Mary's not married, not married . . . .

Even Degas envied her line,
her spareness: only one or two colors

appear in her Japanese prints.

I have a deep bowl filled with gravel and bulbs,
hyacinths, stalks

of white stars exploding
disturbing perfume, and I stake them

and love them to death, whatever that means
about love, and passion, and grudge.

LANDSCAPE

The dove's song, a country song, some sadness or other,
sounds from the telephone wire above the soft lawn and the gravel drive.

I walk away from it, down to Ruby's fruit and tomato stand
and into the sun of a day still summer, dusty berries everywhere.

I walk all morning until I can't hear it, past the tree farm and the store
where they sell tractors and weed whips, and up the big hill

to the intersection, cars coming; sometimes it makes me breathless
to see how ugly the road becomes with the weedy stuff

cut away for black macadam. I stop up there
talking stories to myself of houses never to be dismantled

and slick and watery places silent except for the reeds.
Walking to a crossroads and walking home is my life's

business with some humming hornets and wasps in it,
fields and leaves. My friend is sick. *Coah, cooo, cooo, coo.*

EARLY WINTER

You were dying and I loved the rain.
I loved the houses darkened by the rain,

the Greek contours, sculpted and voluptuous,
of naked trees across the road.

I loved the ancient gods persisting.

All I saw: limbs of elm the rain soaked, sky
a kind of silver, were graceful

like contemplative humanity,
like the city, gauzy in the rain.

I bought a plate, blue Staffordshire, blue
imperiled world: manor, cattle, and white roses

identical to the kind you grew: *Pascali.*

Everywhere: ecstatic woods, abundant
grief like breath inside the rocks.

I loved the rain and the road was wet; the road was black.

"BRIEFLY IT ENTERS AND BRIEFLY SPEAKS"

it is hard to look at him since
he lost perspective and the world
grew flat as if it had spun backwards to
1491 the timbers of the Santa Maria
were black boughs still because it rained so often
it is hard to be what they wish of me
up here immune to torment I had such
instruction in the tedium of pain

I remember yellowing a long time in my
cotton shift until the end when God elected me
to die suffering more pointedly
whiter clearly bloodless
everything clamping down to work
the iron boot the Catherine wheel

it is a terrible thing a terrible thing

he ties his shoes he walks toward edges
of horizon I want him looking
near the center all the bodies children rivers
flowering apple Spanish moss
he'd see the summoned concentration
it takes to be the wind in hemlocks in the pines
on the pond I am the reef and reef again
of riffled water joy or tempered joy

FOUR FRIENDS

For Bob, Louis and Louise

First the easy traffic of the wind,
the down-shifting air on the pond of importunate geese,
all of them painted like geese, grey and black on the
grey-green water, and the soft, wet air, the girlish air
patterning the whole day which was already weightless;
likewise without solidity was the landscape of low berry bushes,
and oaks the only verticals.

      Inside the rented house
were objects none of us owned, a scarred table,
a broken bureau, nothing to yoke us at all.

On that Sunday, whoever had drifted and been let go,
whoever had burdened themselves
with wishes, all of us
      small angels
sat there talking
nothing but a mood like post World-War II anticipation
that wasn't aerospace or washing machines but simple
confidence where the sun shone; the Arctic daybreak
couldn't be seen; not everything was possible.

DEPOSITION

The whole world or the one soul, difficult figures in my divided thinking,
called out like a star on a cloudy night: *see me, see me unique* —

In dreams, the small amounts of logic I possessed grew smaller:
my house was not my house but a thousand different houses.

And in the many rooms, the dead governed all the living,
and in the well-fixed window light I heard

the light commanding: *look out, look out,*
                                        which I took to be a warning.

There were many moods thoughout the rooms;
there was everything there was — perilously sheltered —

Outside, the white, voiceless houses
appeared constant and impossibly the same, the yews

on many lawns stood joining, despite the creek and asphalt road.
        Beside that road I saw some stones resembling opening roses.

Under one sky, blue noon, I picked a rose of composite stone.

II

BRIEF

The drawing called the universe,
look at it closely,
what you see is blue sky
below which the earth wears its many colors.

And the lights springing up like flowers on the earth,
they are cities
speckled with gold, with dirty rain,

so much commerce, even in the countryside.

And anywhere you look, everywhere you look,
lovers touch each other, and how gentle they appear,
how sensitive their fingers are
tracing a name at the nape of a neck, on a nipple, a cheek.

You could perish with sorrow thinking
so much love will end
with all the interfering problems
that never have solutions

except abandonment,

you could just lie down
despairing for those lovers
in one of the light green fields.

As for us, we will not be harmed by sadness.

Even on the larger canvas, eternity,
I see you with me, always
on blazing fire, the anger between us never dying

down.

THE COLLUSION

for Gary Short

Once they were young
which is not to say more innocent,
only less assured: their falterings were painful.

That habit they had of dreaming
and pulling the dreaming around them
like a tent,

        oh, weren't they excitable, half-
speechless,
        and then they pinned down love; listen
to those cries —
          Sheer joy?

Who's to know
what those bodies leaning into namelessness
meant to say until it was bright
daylight?
        And then they saw all the leaves had fallen,
all the green ferns withered.

They made a pact: they would keep alive
something of their former lives
even if it hurt them,

something of the rage, the Romantic pyre —

VINEYARD

Casa is for house and house is for the body
and body is the ocean at beautiful Lucy Vincent beach.

I stood there breathing in. At the beach that nears Menemsha,
I saw scavenging, gritty gulls, poor golden-footed gulls,

saw cliff swallows looping and returning.
And the roses looked like pillows — big and full —

the candle-colored roses were as cool and wide as basins
in the house, silken roses day and night.

At dawn I heard the towhees.
There were purple stones throughout Menemsha,

and shrubs, and many trees. I had my Field Guide,
my paradox, my wooden bridge of now and then:

I remembered when I kept a memory of my father
dying even as he breathed. *He* had his stricken soul

and I knew him for a broken house,
a sullen, reckless man. Reckless was the loneliness.

House of canary yarrow,
I was a ghost but so was everyone.

Lonely was the body, even as it looked
for love, a flimsy, tender wing on water.

I touched my husband's upper arms.
So much desire, so much willful chicory and luxury.

I tasted salt and peaches. The wind was soft. I slept.

NEW ADDRESS

In my region, with its strips of brown and green
and heaven right above,

when the lovesick beg,

the rain and sunlight are like solace
coming down, money

to fund the soothing shoots of applewood.

And the corn-dance frenzy, the waltzing
in spangled, black boleros,

what are they but human thanks and offerings?

I see the helpless also sending up their poetry;
seduction is the grammar in those pleas;

people, they all endure such suffering,

such wild, dark illogic.
In their auburn lips: such tremors.

You know, of course, I'm asking for exactly nothing.

Isn't that good?

Do you want to give it to me now?

TO HEAVEN

I wished you loved me. My husband did;
he lay down and told me

his explicit, sexual dreams,

and there were naked girls with us, and boys,
fishermen most likely,

because of their tans, and nets.

Thus he and I roamed Sicily: the ruins and Etna
on view from our hotels —

thus the gorgeous story of the body,
                                        lips to mouth —

And the sun shone down on sheep,
their hidden souls on fire

throughout the pasture the light featured in so prominently

along with hawks and whitened grass
and coarsest flowers copying our ardor

by turning toward oblivion

as paradigms of belief: accepting all of everything.

AN OPINION

I think the lovers are beautiful, and brave.

Who knows if the real world thinks this also,
the real world isn't taking any calls,

being occupied inventing thin, crookedly hung doors
opening onto unimagined darkness.

So much terror all around, so much scorn.

The lovers in rooms, February, May,
light of morning streaking the bare floors,

what they know is in the fierce particulars:
cheekbone, hipbone,

flare of ruby on the throat, shuddering
in their bodies, eyes wide open.

A PERSUASION

My gods are so human,
betrayal is poetry to them:

other men, other women —

the dark woman to walk with through Paris,

oh she is beautiful, oh
she hasn't been born,

and the man who is intense
as paradise —

I see how it goes: on the one side,
my figure always ready to believe

in gods, and on the other, those
who are the gods

so human in their want
for the new idea the body —

And the cities and the birch groves,
and birds drinking rain from furrows,

these are distractions
really, different

from the abstract light, being so colossal
it has no reason in the world

to dally, or beguile —

INQUIRY

Remember yesterday's quietness,
when we were the sea, calmed in a white room,

and how torment vanished for a time?

They weren't there, the wind and the great fishes
who disturb the underwater.

Atlantic blue, pale tropical green,
one watery meadow approaching another,

we weren't to be seen in John Lafarge's watercolor
dream of a severed head

floating on a river
with a juxtaposed pink flower.

I knew you didn't like it
when I spoke of lurid things.

What did you object to: terror
absent from a child, adversity

beaten back by wish, or if not that,
then a view of the farthest stars,

and then, the plural oceans, way beyond?

ARGUMENT

Now that there was peace between us

the world occured,
political and sighing

like the ancient Egyptian reliefs,
and also like Vincent Van Gogh

with his poor, oxidizing,
canted solitary story of a bed —

One spent an agitated lifetime
distinguishing one thing from another:

on the list of witnesses: Mr. Fear and Pity.

When we fought the way we did,
sometimes we lay down serenely.

Then we heard the snow, silent messenger.

THE PENALTY

When autumn betrayed most of what they cherished,
they entered a church, reflecting

on the world's disdain: harsh nights
brought wolves to the granite village.

At the cold altar they asked to be redeemed:
their lives were despair

and violation; they asked for a sign
but saw no sign.

Seabirds called above the ocean;
science continued, so did manufacture.

In candlelight these uneasy
human bodies reached for the divine.

It was then they felt intrigue.
Or it was spring, or a feeling like spring:

dare, all
pointed invitation.

PERSPECTIVE

     The lower field filled
with evanescent birds

in peril in the old grass. Already,
I grieved at your departure

because I could not think
how to subvert the end.

But the birds, they were a sure felicity.

And the sun,
and the great and lighter rains,

they were perpetual,

to say nothing of the polished cat
suspended

at the field's edge
     in a plume of silence —

INTERPRETATION

I saw the treeline from the center
of the southern field, the great oaks

disturbed by daily wind, the leaves
each day losing so much sustenance.

I saw the universal world of autumn:
fire, descent, and the blind

sympathetic moles
digging into toughening earth,

gravedigger moles in the graveyard.

Such small bits to anguish over.

What I witnessed was a remedy
to chaos, a correction

for some ruthless lilacs that overran their beds.

And the sensual calls of birds
telling a story that ended, *good-bye* —

by now those birds were bound to dusk:
that agent of mystery, all tactics, really,

and mouth.

HER TESTIMONY

All night I saw him
lie down with himself; all night
his hard, closing door closed

tight, winter tight, a dreamt cold
around him, a live razor
wire on him like, that companion of my bed,
a shirt of mail, glistering.

I wanted the invention of bodies
out in the gleaming
beginning, wanted

heaven on earth,
and was this a crime, this eagerness;
was my punishment anger:

on the blue and white dinner plates suddenly
there was so much to swallow: the moon
through the window, another's will;

for instance, I don't remember the exact
moment of betrayal when I learned
faithlessness was the silence
he called blessed

solitude and I called silence
like when children are awake in rooms
all night alone.

CONFUSED FIGURE

One of many, the exhilarated heart,
it was supposed to find kinship
with a sum of hearts,

and absolve itself from isolation.

Spring showed up with sun
to contain the snow

and it was March, struggling
muddy March, without
the potency of summer;

the sparrows anyway continued;
the bulbflowers rose with difficulty

and I was overwhelmed

by men and women, diverse yet in agreement,
and a climax forest: pine and pine and pine.

I didn't know what I understood.

I colluded once with you
to become the absolute same body.

And there was joy in that agreement
even though, snagged
above us in the maple,

the idea of separate selves
appeared singularly beautiful,

so distinctive was its panic, and desire —

GARDEN IN THE FIELD

Of course it's easy to want plenty
and the mess that comes with it

when it isn't complicated
with a wish for order. For instance,
I wanted the rakes in an obedient row;

I wanted even the dirt — subdued —

Planted in lines, one small blue flower
was enough to surprise me; the yellow anthers
made a sun and mimic sky.

But it wasn't enough to stay tidy
when desire called out — coupled with vertigo —

for everything flamboyant, everything luscious:
at dusk you entered the garden
with precise hands, and a body of knowledge.

THE DOVE

I let him go; I released him
at one of God's airports,

the dun and the blue of him —

He was late; he was busy;
like his deceased cousins,

the carrier pigeons,
he had deliveries to make, news to bring

of my restive species, and sky —

He was as light as I imagined him,
a man like any man,

trying for the intimate
in the language of Cortez.

He called me Constance, *girl-of-Mexico*.

Poor bird, he knew I practiced falsehood
in the shadows; that is why he mourned;

he knew exactly how I loved him,
bird-of-the-moon, wild bird

high up in ether, mote-bird, speck
and wingéd agent

dissolving in the air —

THE DIFFERENCE

He put his book away.
I was in the book.

He closed his eyes so he could see me
as he thought I was. That summer,
I saw what I imagined;

I saw him.

When he put the book away,
he had me read the book
that stirred his body.

Dismissive of the figure in the present,
what did he desire?

He said, distant memory.
In sleep: *once and long ago* . . .

There was darkness
when I closed my eyes
and saw what he desired, and heard

an angel shut a door.
I panicked thinking of that angel

he was right to want to see;
he searched for paradise

to press against his lips, paradise
to fuse his soul
with white: integrity.

I knew we had no future.

COUNTERPOINT

That woman, that narcotic.
That beautiful woman making an art

of her Spartan room. Maybe she
put one flower in there.

Next to her bed: one dotted lily.

I admit she was clever, standing out
against nothing. Men went for that.

On my brown barn, climbing roses,
Aloha, so many pink incidentals,

brilliant as finches yesterday evening, finches
like pieces of gold: preserved, medieval

clans come for the summer
and already drunk in the white flowers.

Peonies. So many big flowers.
I stood there: "Fierce and alone."

"Fierce and alone."

BRIEF

Not choosing is a fearful way.
My fingers agree; they touch.
My fingers touch the table
and once I chose the table
and the chair; once I caressed the fabric
of the chair and was excited
by the feel of the cloth. The lamp?
I picked it out to compliment the dusk.
I saw it: old and therefore holy. I saw it was
Chinese: intaglio of lotus at the base.
The lamp was green
like the ocean somewhere south of here.

I chose this northern plot.
I couldn't leave the house
and the light inside, and the stone
foundation: granite apparent now
that the plantings are all gone. I paid a man
to dig and haul them, poor dark yews,
somebody else's choice, and I'm not sorry.
I'm thinking of men and women comparing
this one's shoulders with that one's
silky belly. I imagine what they think:
I never choose; I'm never lonely.
They are only wrong and coughing
in their beds like owls, like poets,
the great, ecstatic crazies.

I've chosen to be harsh.
Now that you've left you know this;
now you unbutton your shirt
in rooms south of here.
There was no elegance left and I was shouting.
I stood near the washing machine and dryer.
Catbirds fought in the hemlock.

I wanted liberty imbedded in desire, but
a girl pounding clothes on rocks
was the one you dreamed swaying
like a swimming fish entering your net
suspended from the riverbank. Such pliancy
and quiet. It was sweet, the silence. Over and over,
I woke us up. I was righteous; I woke us up.

STATEMENT

How heavy you came to be, beloved.

Last spring, redoubtable
tulips — my choice, actually, for joy —

quivered like language
emerging from the dark

while your tread anticipated
that very dark with force,

it seemed, and pleasure.

You were always that way:
deep and contained

like an urn made to receive
thick spokes of tulips, and ashes.

My leaded darling, my titan,

even the trees grew still
as your weight passed over them.

I was no ignorant flower.

I flung you hard
from my outstretched hand.

III

TOO YOUNG

I'm too young, too girlish, have not enough
sureness on the podium
where I'm clearing my throat,
don't know the answer, and I buy
my roses on Gano Street for ten dollars a dozen
if anyone asks. So many years of young,
so many years of playing with the dog
not Chekhov's tiny one exhausted
on the woman's thighs
but a golden, jumpy, toothy dog
too young to know the sanctity of chickens.
My love and I, we had some chickens once
when the beans rose high as temple pillars
and the vines sang Greek! Greek!
That year of the intimate, the man that year
was greedy for my imagination.
                                        Greek! Greek!
And Paris, Paris, France!
Taking up the chickens, one laid blue eggs,
and two, who died on top of feed sacks
in great and endless heat, looked like Elvis
in headdress, Elvis-Indian-chickens.
Take me to the Badlands
where creepy Parkman took his notes, was crazy
for the death of things; I'll never care for Boston.
There is one rose on my bedroom table;
I've been lying down; I've been recovering;
I've been told no again, no like the north,
like a lie. Take me to the rose,
to the green girl of the flower;
take me to the holy mass of petals
shaking in a draft; loose me
in the wind; take me to the pleasure boat
soon to sail from the harbor, from the lights —

THE WEDDING

America and trains, wasn't it so?

Train men, union men,
ghosts in the weeds the tracks

flattened out, topic of songs
kids sang all summer,

wasn't it that, wouldn't you say?
And horses from the territories

of Spanish Arizona.

November once, wasn't it clear,
you turkey, you assassination,

that you thought-you-saw-Joe-Hill-last night

working on the railroad?

Wouldn't you laugh
at the *freedom* of the vote,

at backroom wackos,
the Artichoke Party, the Bread Basket

Caucus, likewise laugh at *Wild Love*,
a technicolor flick

of the poet shooting up,
and nuns outside the door,

sex and nuns, how charming
blonde Italian, wouldn't you guess,

how American train, how rackety
carriage, how Caribbean slave-trade

flowers on the floor, how whisk-broomed
time, how filtered cigarette,

how grief and yes married like that?

ONLY A STORY

Though you had been fooled before, believe me
the white dress was never a blue, not even a twilight blue
that covers the rabbits; the dress had no touches of lilac;
rabbits rested near lilacs; believe me the fabric was French
but the brilliant merchant-designer Jacquard
set no loom for the cloth, nor yelled in his mill,
this floor is filthy; he was long ago buried and dead.
Death is the song some poets sing and the song is a charm
for the body. The dress wasn't the body. Simply cut,
beautifully stitched, it laughed at the logic of therefore:
the dress is white: the cow is white: the white cow is the dress.
You grew up with that thinking: so nervous.

In a thousand years, in Paradise, you'll be
slipping the dress over your head, letting it
fall down your shoulders, the whole cling of it
a lovemaking skein of notorious, ethical, silken desire.
You already know the body's singleness
a ghost's *remember me, remember me* calls out against.
You are not splinters of an immigrant boat or boxes
of brisket and Schubert the sun bears down on, my God!
You see the Gerald Stern original waiting for the dead
William Carlos Williams to come across the Hudson,
not the Jordan. And you are never Eve. Even in Paradise
you wear a white dress and she is only a story.

PURELY DRINKING MY COFFEE

for Joseph Landers

I am a leaf or bird today I am so happy.
I fly to the station of Bliss, I know
all of Wallace Stevens, all the baseball stats,
my cheeks are red from the cold,
my feathers puff-up with the cold, my veins are
crackling, I perch on grey-blue granite,
on billboards promoting spring cruises,
my vanished parents sail on the *Queen Mary*
and dine with Wallace and Mrs. Stevens,
you know she posed for the back of the dime,
they trill, they are sparrows, they are singing
azaleas, they are innocent now, they do not send out
for pain, music is in the spheres, snow is falling in Bliss,
an oboe is playing in Bliss for pale Ramon.
I am lifted so high by happiness I cannot see
any three-legged dog, or spittle of rage
or cadre of tyrants, my bloody heart muscle
beats fast, I am a bird, a leaf like all other leaves,
I confuse some information,
Wallace Stevens lays buried with others
who confuse some information, they think
they are lilac sprigs, they think they are
Sunday morning, I am landing and pitching
like Koufax flying like Wallace Stevens,
I have died from indignity: love,
now I am purely drinking my coffee, taking off
my weights, admiring my feathers and color,
I am a ferocious chickadee, a maple leaf, I wear
tortoise-shell reading glasses, dance to the phenomena
of sound, dance and marry wildness to shape.

THE SMALL KILLERS

I wrote a poem called *The Small Killers*.
It was about me and some logical people.
I said they knew Wittgenstein and Keats
and could trace Lewis and Clarke
straight to the ocean and remembered
what Jefferson had to say about Indians and slaves.
I wrote the poem in a cabin in the woods. I played
a Mozart CD. It wasn't logical but I imagined
candles and candelabra, and the hem of my dress
trailing mud in unpaved, eighteenth-century Europe.
I imagined dying in childbirth, and Mozart's dying,
and our shallow graves, and the action of quick-lime.
On February 20th, the first birds I saw
perched on the pines, it was a dark day.
I couldn't tell what the birds were. I wrote
that my reflection obscured them. I thought
I was writing *reflection* with reference to the glass
in the window. Did I really mean *reflection?*
Did I put too much faith in the rhythm of the word?
Logical people wouldn't do that. They would
consult a Roget. They would think of the syntactical
dance of words in a sentence. I wished
I could dance, I wished it was spring. Some of us
would be planting out roses, or driving, or kissing
a baby, or gazing into ozone-fed moods, or marrying,
marrying. Or dreaming a rodeo rider named
Antonio Vivaldi in an American body. Or *any* body.
I realized *reflection* was what I meant. *My reflection
obscured the names of the birds.* Of course. Narcissistic
notation. And here's something else: in the poem
I personified Logic. And I did this because
it was easy. I often hovered near Easy, a river town

above New Orleans. Little Easy. It was warm.
Wisteria bloomed as Jefferson mouldered.
The lights were shot out in the Cotton Exchange.
Since I couldn't tell what the birds were,
I could have said they were peacocks I saw
in the woodland, a fantasy Audubon painting, huge,
that contained all of his birds. They flew and sang
in the squill-studded grass, in the blue bells.
I could have said it was Paradise out there, and nothing
suffered, and that a year ago I didn't scream, *get out,*
to the man who bent over me always in silence.
For years, bending over only in silence. Willfully
lonely. His area, cold mountains.
His animal, the moon.
I was saying, *Truth,* and he was saying nothing.
Not that he didn't have an opinion.
So much chewing. So much thick anger.
Our privacies so rampant. Our hands
in the mud. Our heads hanging down. Empty
spaces, the pelvis, the ribcage. Our dreary sleeping.
Our own humiliations. I made my lists. On the porch
I had my crisis and was full of logic and I stank with fury.

I HAVE HIS LOOK

To the men concerned with angels I say no.

No to their eyes and hands
they hold behind their backs

and no to their heads on stems
bent downward. They walk like rabbis

and like priests, men walking without women.
They look down at grass and stones;

they are encyclopedias: volume "G"
for grass, volume "S" for stone. They tell

the history of stone in Carthage
and in Crete; they tell the goddesses'

attitudes toward lichen-covered stone
and how the sound of "stone" has roots

in some Indo-European river falling down
in rainbow droplets on every iris in the world.

And all that in a walk no more than half a mile.

A man trips, lets go, wrestles
nothing in the dirt

but his very own sad self; angels are elusive;
heaven is elusive; look up, there is nothing

but scrim marked with gulls, clouds, a cry - -

I saw heaven once.
It was a light like many migraines

with black fire at the edges;
I was so excited; I went to see the local holy man.

He was not concerned with angels
but no anyway to him; he was out

for anguish and no smiling,
I like a little levity with my prayers:

a list of natural things
mostly flowers but including

human love which is broken-hearted
bridal wreath and babies breath.

I pray to my smiling blue delphinium
that never lasts for me although I feed the thing

all summer. My husband was also hungry.
He was building us a kitchen; we were young;

all summer we were sweaty
angels; I made him chicken salad;

take off all your clothes, he said.

I hold that time the way I hold a rose;
I twirl that time; it throws

a blue-pink shadow
on the wall like dawn and dusk;

never mind what happened later;
I have his look inside my body, his eyes

like agate blue, shattered vases his poor hands.

AGAINST CLOSING

The legions of near-suicides were not dreaming anything
whereas I was filling up the daylight dreaming,
which I take to mean that dying isn't what I wanted;
change is what I wanted. Storm into rainbow,
chrysalis to butterfly hovering above the wild cherry,
dumb, clarified by conjunction; these are the changes
I wished. Nearby a hedge flowering now
was changing; a robin, wren — some bird —
altered the leaves' configurations
but only for a moment and that is what I liked:
no obvious sustained effect
as in the summertime of imagination
where the field road is dusty and the fields business slow:
bees in knapweed and lace
perpetually moving but not crazy in the tangle.
There wasn't a bee in my family.
When I think about my family interlocking in cold, blue air,
walking to the next town, hurrying to the lights,
some of them actually laughing,
all of them not in the field, I feel lonely
for the traffic that they liked, the hurly-burly
silks and nervousness. The thick album
where they hurry through so many blurred pictures
is sad enough to hollow me.
I think about their eagerness; I think about their cars.
The other day I watched a movie
where a boy is harmed so casually and often
that he starts to run. Five minutes running, running
in the scrub, running to the sea; the film doesn't end; it stops.

MY LITTLE ESPERANTO

The dirt-and-grease-and-brown-rose-rot-Community-Garden-woman-
out-of-the rice-paddy-with-Toltec-baby-on-the-back-
party begins, good morning, like a tiger, a lullaby on the dirge-cusp,
and is gorgeous, not ever sitting one minute, not a moment insouciant,
and absolutely lagging badly in the calm department, carrying life around
in an iron hand-cart-with-peony, and a thousand people a second attend,
drinking *elixirs*, essence-of-nutrient-flavor, no-fat-bubbled-up-*juices*,
and all of the guests as troubled and as lithe as cats
and as lonely as any human dog. And all of them talking
rare-specimen-of-horticulture-talk and sparrow-gabble.
They have matches in their pockets and two books: *Faust*, translated
by the neighborhood Buddha, the tricky one, and another book I forget.
They talk love language in couplets, in near-tears, in the soft sounds
called love sounds that I love; beautiful sheets they wear, beautiful laundry.
There's a child with an old greenish-metal elephant that was a valentine;
another child has some marbles shiny with good-bye, but no one is thinking
of going yet; it's only afternoon, maybe it's later but *just*. Listen, the last time
you kissed me, yesterday, did you think you had me then? You had me then.
You had me like this party I'm having, this immaculate tinsel, this irony,
this Homeric tradition with salt, this disorder, this groveling, this splaying
and rapture; sweetheart, the silence will be awful when we die and leave.

Note

"Briefly It Enters And Briefly Speaks" is a title of a poem by Jane Kenyon.